# Critical Standpoint

Documentation on the Coronavirus
coming from two epicenters

Raheem Cox

Printed in the United States of America

Author: Raheem Cox
Edited by: Million Dollar Pen, Ink

ISBN: 979-8-218-01403-2

# Dedication

Dedicated to my father, Paul Cox, brother, Rashid Cox, and my niece and nephew, Ava & Rashid Cox JR

# TABLE OF CONTENTS

Introduction...................................................vii

Chapter 1 ........................................................1
Diamond Princess, Arrival of Coronavirus to N.Y, Jail within a jail

Chapter 2 ........................................................8
Economic depletion, Prison spread, Predisposed backgrounds

Chapter 3 .......................................................14
Epicenter, Governing politics

Chapter 4 .......................................................20
Remote learning, Possible medical relief, Devastation in Africa

Chapter 5 .......................................................26
Congressional assistance, The homeless, unemployment

Chapter 6 .......................................................32
School closings, Business shutdowns, and stay-at-home orders

Chapter 7 .......................................................36
Our experts silenced, Experimental vaccine

Chapter 8 .......................................................41
Minority communities, Why not reopen

Chapter 9 .......................................................46
George Floyd, Steps towards reopening, Summary of myself

Afterword.......................................................53

# Introduction

The pathogenic disease termed COVID-19 was initially marked as home to China. By the time this disease slowed down, and the governing call for release was issued, the amount of those infected throughout the United States was over a soaring number of 1,000,000. With over 100,000 deaths in response to it. At first, overhearing talk on T.V about COVID-19, I wasn't too levitated toward a deep concern about it. Seeing that our last two viruses that played a toll on this country, the Swine flu and Ebola, didn't play a major role in the casualties of death. But soon afterward, I took heath to its devastation.

At the height of the pandemic, deaths were occurring at a rapid rate of 700 to 800 people daily for the epicenter in cases (New York City). Which was, by all means, a problem, if not fixed, would move normal Americans into government-funded camps to be properly contained. I can assure you that all age-bearing groups of America were stunned to know their peace and tranquility would so swiftly be interrupted. Another factor, there is no guarantee this margin won't return following the release. Those atop our government say Coronavirus will be here years after its entrance (Feb 2020).

Diseases similar to the one we are facing is nothing uncommon surrounding worldly endeavors. There has been a dark history of the formation of plagues throughout the world. From the black death in the 14th century. To the plague in London 300 years later. To the Spanish flu, which was over 100 years ago.

Of a person and as a writer, I have always been definitive, a trait you shall view in this writing that I consider to be a booklet that can be shared down the generations. If one day this virus is brought to a cease. Within the content, you will find two to four important accounts from each chapter emphasizing what most importantly shaped news coverage of Coronavirus, mainly in New York City but also internationally. It also provides you with a look into my holding confinements, Which shows skill in formatting. Most chapters end off with NYC summarizing stats to make clear dictation of the rise and fall of Coronavirus- until the release: Total hospitalized, Those hospitalized in last 24 hours, Total cases, cases in last 24 hours.

Where was I positioned at the break of this crisis? Elmira State Correctional Facility. Yes, I was serving time on a 13-year bid in which I was a year and a half short to go home. As I gathered more intel about the virus, I then knew it would be much more of an overwhelming crisis than I was held to believe. As panic rose, also I was fastened knowing those on the outside were too much in burden to have the settlement in covering a complete story that would soon be recorded as one of the greatest atrocities in American history. The testimony of this booklet I consider to be a [critical standpoint] of when the virus first arrived in the U.S to the time reopening began for states abroad. Though months exceeding the reopening, there was a second wave that caused an even more disastrous role in the disease charted COVID-19 for many states in this country. I took on the role in aiding in readable documentation simultaneously to the prison where I resided, becoming the epicenter for infected inmates, with over 475 infected. So know I'm not just laying out information that didn't cause me any negligence. I believe this booklet serves its purpose. And as a reader, I hope you feel welcome to the uniqueness of this presentation, which was completed as an eyewitness behind bars to be of public view; a vivid recital of just how hectic the times where you were scrambling and worrying if you were fortunate enough to pull through as a survivor of this disease. Because there are many missing links and the fight over this disease is sill in the works, the introduction was not meant to be lengthy. My honest opinion of the overall completion of the text is that it was better documented than how ABC covered their footage from beginning to reopening.

# Chapter 1

Diamond Princess, Arrival of Corona to N.Y,
Jail within a Jail, Stimulus package.

What was meant to be a family getaway turned direction and was publicized as the first iconic view Americans gained attention towards a deadly virus that could possibly head their way. It was February 16, 2020. News made way a cruise ship named the Diamond Princess had been docked since February 5th under quarantine in Yokohama, Japan, after being found out that a recent passenger from Hong Kong tested positive for the Coronavirus (COVID-19).

What an awful way to ruin a vacation. One of the passengers aboard the ship Sarah Arana spoke on this dreadful 2-week quarantine as "frantic." Out of the 3,500 people on board, 285 aboard tested positive within 10 days. Among this cruise liner, there were 380 Americans. As days went by, people were growing highly frustrated.

Those that chose not to return (Americans) on the charter flight were warned they will be unable to get back to the U.S for a period time. A reminder to all that international play can make a governance great and also has the ability to inflict harm upon. To mention, before the incident on the ship occurred worldwide, the infection rate was already at 70,000, with most of the cases in China.

A pathogen which is defined- as an agent causing disease- in this event is the deadliest disease 21st century America has ever faced. Even more harmful than AIDS. WHY? The majority of those exposed to this disease catch it through the air. Making it unavoidable in a high populated area, as seen by the devastation it would later play in the epicenter of America, New York City. Before the 9-11 crisis and up until now, America has been looked at as a safe haven with vast superiorities in technology and building structure that has been accessible for the comfort of those within. With deadly viruses coming and going throughout the past decade, I *don't* believe Americans had any idea what was soon to come.

As of Monday, February 17, the crisis aboard the ship grew more extreme as 450 people tested positive for Coronavirus. Making it the largest center of infections outside China. Of those that were stricken by the virus, there were 46 Americans. These forty-six Americans didn't have the opportunity to fly back to their homeland. While 340 Americans flew back. Among them, there were 14 that tested positive. The coverage of this news article is what opened my cautionary senses as I was informed of the swiftness in spreading COVID-19 was capable of. This was also around the time where things were getting "stewing" here at my correctional facility, as postage were on the walls, and gossip was being relayed from inmate to inmate that there is a possibility us in our holding confinements were under possible circumstances of "sitting ducks" if this thing got too far out of control.

My hometown New York City would soon become -and kept the title all throughout this crisis- the epicenter weeks following the dilemma aboard the Diamond Princess. Statewide there were 613 cases. Gov. Cuomo announced around this point that of the six-hundred thirteen, there were 269 in the city of New York. In a place like the rotten apple, many don't consider things a threat until things are in front view of them. It should be recognized that at this margin of outbreaks, Mayor DeBlasio was of unsuitable assistance while he kept public schools open amid the quickly spreading virus even as the second Staten Island student tested positive.

Gov. Cuomo gave his input, saying the rising number of positive cases was a good thing. Because it sectioned those diagnosed in quarantine and away from the general public. Give or take not bad advice.

With many in fear due to schools staying open, which I can assure you our Mayor would later regret. DeBlasio suggested he had the Publics well-being at heart by refusing to close the nation's largest school system. I believe our Mayor was concerned with the amount of kids without close monitoring. Meanwhile, our experts, by this time, should have already illustrated the severances of improper social regard to this wild uproar that would be considered a pandemic weeks later.

March was a month of mayhem for communities around the U.S. For businesses, our prison system, and the strain of our governing body. The Rapid rate of infection is what scared me the most. By March 23, the forgotten souls of our prison system parted, coinciding in jail within a jail. Riker's lsland is a holding center where inmates are between a request to go home and a sentence to an upstate correctional facility. Already predisposing them to being [edgy].

By March 23, the forgotten souls were the headline of concern by what was now labeled a pandemic. Contagion amongst inmates was the main concern issue. How would you like to be confined anywhere where you were under the assumption that your close-by fellow inmate has a deadly disease. This was the case by this period as 29 inmates and 17 DOC employees were now positive on Riker's Island. For those in jails where the infection rate was more than 10, I believe they were hit the hardest.

Truly my heart goes out to the staff at Riker's as they were bent out of shape with a problem that was grueling and condition frustrating. They were forced to prolong with normal procedures meanwhile reckon with the fear of losing their jobs. Let it be known Rikers's Island is far from equipped to brace a circumstance like COVID-19. The equipment needed as I glanced through television notice was out of reach. Later mention in this booklet will yield the staff at Riker's and just how un-caring and un-giving the situation for prison staff was so exempt during this pandemic.

This period in the pandemic was also of great turmoil for workers. The Labor Department reported 3.3 million unemployment claims across the country at this point. Forcing thousands of businesses to be left vacant, leaving millions of workers with no way to collect a paycheck.

Many of our governing body to the people across the United States gave poor initial response to the rigorous insight of Coronavirus. I believe some laid poor instruction unintentionally and intentionally. Just by how far off their opinion was. Donald Trump is one of them. I do appraise Trump and both chambers of Congress for being of desperate aid to the people at the closing of March for compensation of the devastation Coronavirus caused. By this point, the spread of the bug cases was above 100,000.

The bill was a relief to millions of workers, companies, and state governments plummeting down financial deficit. The bill was a 2.2 trillion dollar rescue package. 2.2 TRILLION DOLLARS! Being an American, I must be in good hands. "That's only if the bug doesn't get a hold of me." It bankrolls directly payments of up to 1,200 to most taxpayers, bolsters unemployment benefits, provides loans, grants, and tax breaks to small and large businesses, and funnels billions into state government coffers and the nation's health care system.

While many were suffering dearly, this bill leveled the playing field. A bill of this scaling amount was never administered for U.S. citizens. With that type of money, you can buy an adjacent earth #2.

As an inmate, steps toward progress in this event in American history were shaping up. Meanwhile, as a detainee, I along with other inmates, were still a lost cause. Throughout the city, by March 30, city jails were infested with the Coronavirus, ranging up to 800 infected. The majority of those were held at Riker's. 350 in total. To serve as a sign based on new arrests, approved releases, and other factors, the Correction Department and Correction Health Services did not have control on the outbreak.

To make things more clear, when you are in a situation where you're being monitored by a staff member that hates his job just as much as you hate your stay in a jail facility, apply a circumstance like a fast spread virus within, and then picture the view of things.

By March 30 here in Elmira Correctional Facility, signs were being bannered on the wall displaying what the coronavirus was and how to avoid chances of being affected by it. My cell was becoming stock piled with newspapers as I sought out material I desired for this writing. My contact back at home after a visit, previously brought to my attention corona is more severe of a disease than our last Ebola.

# Chapter 2

## Economic depletion, Prison spread, Predisposed backgrounds

Steering towards April 3 is when the economy of America went on a chaotic depletion. As scarcity in jobs became the new wave with more than 6.6 million applying for benefits. Giving stroke to the nature of this catastrophe, stating that if strategic implementations weren't made quickly, we could be looking at a final end to America.

The type of descent waged at our country was a deep recession, with nearly 10 million workers laid off within 2 weeks. A kind of drop that up until present times has not been recorded on a national scale. Was this even more plummeting of a fall than the great depression of the 1930s? Yes. During the 1930's it took 3 and a half years to go from full unemployment in 1929 to 25% unemployment in 1933. The wave of the Coronavirus has put on a showcase of full employment to depression in 3 and a half weeks.

The comfort zone for many of the Big Apple has not been tampered with so crudely since our last recession of 2009. Overall technological improvement in our nation has almost wiped out the pitfalls of such a harsh crisis. The saying goes, "expect the unexpected."

Deplorably speaking, many of our officials high above admitted that they didn't combat the public health crisis properly from the beginning. Which would have defeated the need to implement social distancing.

And this can be known better told by the blatant truth that the feds waited until mid-March to begin making bulk orders of ventilators, N95 respirators, masks, and other supplies that New York officials so dearly needed. Mid-March! Don't be surprised if controversy behind the handling of COVID-19 dose leak for the following years.

Back to home for criminals in New York City, things were lawfully disastrous. In a span of a week, 441 Correction Department staffers and 287 in custody were hit by Coronavirus (covid- 19) by April 9. Thats just part of the distress. DOC personnel took upon their jobs to oversee and counsel offenders of the law within their positioned facilities - I believe. And under already a department that is the [register] of law, they should be of comfort knowing first that due to their job title, if things got out of control, they are superseded by the right administration.

Coincidentally many officers working in Riker's were forced to work triple fours, missing meals, and sent to work on their free days. Even more unsanctionable officers who tested positive, out sick, and who still showed symptoms were told by the [the Health Management Division] at DOC they should come back to work. What a shame.

Even as their doctors made regards as it being unsafe. Ironically, the DOC states the health and safety of its officers are their #1 priority. Not to put all the torment on the DOC and its handling of its officers, the Coronavirus targeted many groups in this country. It laid an effect on workers, business owners, students in need of education, and even particular ethnic backgrounds.

The ethnic background most victims to this crisis within a crisis are African-Americans. Who are predisposed to diabetes, hypertension, obesity, and asthma. Making their chances of dying from it far greater due to the fact that those with these illnesses cannot fight off the pathogen as opposed to someone in a normal health status. Another exposure risk is that blacks are likelier to work at jobs regarded as essential vice those able to work from a safe home environment.

Luckily my counselor here was very informative himself on the virus and the spread of corona in which by April, 9 he in a weekly meeting we have together let me know corona had played a bigger role almost in fatalities than the entire Vietnam war in America. That's when I became a little more alert as I called my contact on the outside. My contact let me know three older men I once knew growing up were killed by corona.

April, 13, 2020

New York City corona virus stats

Total cases: 104,410          Cases in last 24 hours: 6,182

Total deaths: 6,182          Deaths in last 24 hours: 440

Total hospitalized: 27,676

# Chapter 3

## Epicenter, Governing politics

Small notations in preventive status, along with a throw out of guiding instruction for the people to me, is what shaped the rise of infection and death rates around the U.S. So, if I were to suggest just why the U.S death toll passed Italy, making it the world's highest going on mid-April, or why my hometown New York became the epicenter of the disease, I can only base my opinion on my minimum source of resources. Being incarcerated at the time of this outbreak, I did have communication with those on the outside that helped me along understanding the faults of such a pandemic and who was mournfully at blame.

My intentions for putting this booklet together was for the usage of those that were highly worrisome at the break of this virus and would like to have coverage of the entirety of this crucial situation.

Through experience by any in an affair when a virus of no charted out origin of appearance claims the lives of more than a thousand victim's skepticism over if it was the consequence of natural or unnatural occurrence will emerge. I was a little unsatisfied by the handling from a watchful eye over the aid given by our governmental administrations. Nationwide, hearing so many misconceptions from them left me curious of the original formation of the bug.

The U.S death toll by mid-March reached a higher rate than that of Italy. Taking the lives of more than 20,000. While Italy stood at 19,648. Around this period, New Yorkers were stricken in death by the bug at a fatal measure of 700 deaths daily. As I mentioned, the charting behind the virus was of suspicion. China, where the virus began last year, was given speculation due to low reported cases it documented. Already being credited as the home to the virus with fewer than 85,000 infections

Meanwhile, the U.S recorded more than 500,000. About 29% of the worldwide count. "Fishy."

I stand neutral, though, in the debate over how it formed, knowing its origin by the time you receive this booklet will be swayed in many different alterations and statements formulizing just how it began. I encourage you to read this controversial write-up from beginning to end. Being that through it you will be of great awareness, assisting you in day by and week by weekly encompassment, narrowing down your eagerness to know how this all began.

Pre-Coronavirus, I condoned the practice of Mayor DeBlasio and Governor Cuomo being New York's body of governing support. Do I agree with every detail of their political practice? No. In a position like theirs, where it already takes a suitable age to be of adaptation and a trendy and lengthy profile to serve under such people, ordinary supervision is already a big shoe to fill. So why did New York City become the epicenter? Hard to say

The blame by many is being directed at DeBlasio and Cuomo for muffling the threat level initially and hesitating to take precautionary steps. How would you like to tell a mass crowd of arrogant snotty people - under new policy- they are now banned from mass gatherings, closing of schools and businesses, issue them stay at home orders and require them the use of face masks. By all means, though, through prior data at hand, unfortunately, they should have acted sooner.

New York City culture itself rectifies a cause totally opposite of provisions to be secluded. Speaking on their population density is extremely difficult to practice social distancing in large apartment buildings, crowded sidewalks, and packed subway cars.

Mid- April was when preventive status started to become more apparent here in Elmira. Classes were canceled along with vocational training, and the wearing of face mask were evident by correctional officers and counselors. There also became no movement. Being locked down all day without a way to vent was highly frustrating.

April, 18, 2020

New York City corona virus stats

Total cases: 122,148          Cases in last 24 hours: 4,583

Total deaths: 12,199          Deaths in Iast24 hours: 722

Total hospitalized: 32,843

# Chapter 4

## Remote learning, Possible medical relief, Devastation in Africa

As this country is split apart in employment, distribution of currency, service availability and schooling standards, one of the most neediest concerns is for students to be handled correctly, being that they are in dire want to make it to the next grade. There's something that is certain by the crisis we are under, these young shapers of our country know a crucial standpoint in the importance of the branches of our economy and their key function.

After the seventh week of remote learning and following the announcement when DeBlasio mentioned schools would stay closed for the academic year, a new entry was put into course in which traditional grades would be dropped for all city public students except high-schoolers. Without conventional learning, there had to be some new implementation that would teach these mass of students.

How this will be handled more discreetly is for students from kindergarten through fifth grade, modem practice of evaluation will be replaced by a "meets standard" or "Needs improvement." And the core replacement backing this new cut-out will be online academia. DeBlasio covered the new plan by stating it would be an evaluation of three particular categories - school projects, assignments, and writing entries -which will be assigned online.

The effort to reach a system of determining who stays behind and who moves on shows that New York schooling is durable and something in place for a crisis that can promote diplomacy for our students. This being the first event in my life where this was needed, me as a high school graduate, also I feel more safeguarded parentally for the future of my kids.

The battle we and our government are under at this given time is tedious. Never, since the great depression of the 30s, has there been such an assessment of teamwork throughout to keep our country stable. Everyone has to play their part. I'm glad that ways to carry into effect each day to get America back up and running are on the way. And that as a witness to such a catastrophe for future reference, we as a people will know by an experience a crucial lesson in adjusting and adapting to regain the pride and glory of what many look at as the greatest country on earth.

The first sign of medical relief in fighting off this pathogen was publicized late April. Announcing an experimental drug that works against the Coronavirus. Word got around that government officials would work to make it of usage to the people as soon as possible. This new drug manufactured by Gilead Sciences named Remdesivir has a promising effect on patients contacted by COVID-19. Coming from a study of 1,063 patients, Remdesivir halted the time recovery by 31%.

An average of 11 days verse 15 for those given usual care. The Study of the drug needs further study. It also might be reducing deaths. What has been found now is that a drug can block the virus. It has a clear effect. With 226,000 people worldwide fatally struck, the time is now for our pharmaceutical care to turn Coronavirus from a list of battles to a war won by medical remedy.

Without substantial overall testing of this drug, I'm sure most Americans would take it as a suggestion for the sake of a better possibility. And if this new drug shortened the recovery by 31%, I would guess by a study of more length, the same substances within the drug can be examined closer to treat the virus completely.

Being a bit empathetic and not only worrying about American affairs, the continent that is far under grief by this time in world history is Africa. It should be and is already noted by most that Africa's existing conditions of living are a setback to feasible living making them vulnerable to an epidemic similar to covid- 19. Their society is known for overcrowding, unsuitable medical systems, and widespread medical problems. All of which is a magnet for a deadly plague.

By late April, Africa's rate of infection was far beyond Europe's, with more than 18,000 and 550 deaths. Take these numbers cautiously. Their exact charting may be off. The United Nations said Africa could see 300,000 deaths this year. Even administering social distancing and other mediating measures. With how AIDS struck Africa and this virus to me being even more deadly, I would hope other countries can get together and funnel some emergency aid quickly before things get too far out of hand.

Late April was agonizing as there was no let up with all day confinement. Even though I was secluded I still received mail. My contact informed me through postage New York City streets were vacant. And that at his job he was allowed to do work from home. Which was an opportunity for some in New York. At our dining areas where some refer to as mess halls we were ordered to sit one chair after the next.

April, 28, 2020

New York City corona virus stats

Total cases: 156,100          Cases in last 24 hours : 2,896

Total deaths: 16,936          Deaths in last 24 hours: 263

Total hospitalized: 40,050

# Chapter 5

## Congressional assistance, The homeless, Unemployment

I haven't shared the finest experiences with the NYPD or DOC officers. Through humble beginnings and courtesy for those who sincerely wake up every day to protect and serve, I am appreciative that there are those out there that should be credited to their vow of service. It's easy to speak fowl of a police officer or any officer in regards to law enforcement. You must always remember their earnest duties to keep American cities and states jointly upheld, especially in times like these.

Efforts have been attributed to assist in protecting our officers in this given time, but it hasn't been enough. Criminal justice assistance since March by way of Congress has provided 850-million dollars in aid to states and local governments for protective equipment and additional needs, along with 100-million dollars for Federal prisons, who are facing increased infections and deaths and is a highly contagion for virus spread in facilities and in nearby communities. Unfortunately, resources are diminishing quickly.

Reaching May 1 of the virus, 31 members of the NYPD have died. Sickness has strained police departments across the country. Forcing officers to elongate supplies. According to the Bureau of Prison Statistics, by April 23, 620 Federal inmates and 357 staff have tested positive for Coronavirus. Like I mentioned earlier (speaking on prison spread), correction officers and inmates are at a troubling risk in catching the bug due to confined spaces and their close proximity of each other. Our enforcement officers struggle each day to keep us approved from inequality; it is no excuse why they should lack sufficient equipment to protect themselves.

All in all, blabber over what segment or what particular person that is misconstruing liberty and justice, will be cast from beginning to end in the times we are in. Everyone wants things to fit to their acceptance of a harmonized society in the middle of a chaotic pandemic. While I give you feedback on this pandemic, my goal is not to de-foul or lessen the value of any entity in American society without proper cause. I do give props to this country watching things unfold like "storming bees out of a beehive" to a subtle end in climax. Many deserve credit for the downright resistance this virus played on the health of those worldwide.

Stretching towards early May, in a pivotal point for the housing of the homeless, people were dying on the streets, having no place to go. Covid-19 has blanketed the city's tourism trade and general economy. Many hotel owners in reimbursement of cash that they dearly needed were willing to expand homeless programs to a stay by federal grant in their hotels.

The lack of generated revenue almost left them no choice. A normal hotel would make about $10 million to $14 million a year now makes $100,000 from mid March through all of 2020, according to Vijay Dandapini, president of the Hotel Association of New York City. The sad thing is these are the realities in finance for many business owners throughout America. In times like this, new doors open as revenue is deflated.

Stay on your toes, America. A pathogen like this has many counters. Just last month, 4,780 Americans lost their lives to covid-19. Stumbling into the beginning of May, it topped 63,000 fatalities. Long past its peak. Opening for communities around the U.S, to some extent, begins this weekend (May 2). The area of concern in these times that is difficult to compromise with is payment of rent.

In the epicenter of things, tenants gave Cuomo a line of complaints as they are now struggling to pay rent Staging multiple protests around the city and in the state capitol. Talk about the strain of survival. As many suffer economically, Cuomo has denounced his order of barring evictions but has depleted calls for a rent freeze. Tough situation for any governing administration. Approximately 30 million Americans filed for unemployment in the last six weeks, according to the Federal Department of Labor. Lawmakers have proposed a list of bills that would reconcile for this period of anguish but hasn't made anything certain. Making up in the payment of house bills for any city as a whole is difficult. The summary of this, all landlords and building owners who don't receive payment will lead to vacant buildings for both parties (owners and tenants). So how do we fix this problem?

The beginning of May here in Elmira made me think. Mainly due to those I had already lost, and inmates in nearby cells who had themselves family members who died from corona. What if this disease was man made. How will I go about serving under the American flag. And look at all the jobs left unemployed. How will America ever recover?

May, 1, 2020

New York City corona virus stats

Total cases: 162,212                   Cases in last 24 hours: 2,347

Total deaths: 17,866                   Deaths in last 24 hours: 277

Total hospitalized: 41,648

# Chapter 6

## School closing, Business shutdowns, Stay- at- home orders

The Dearing decision by mid-March, administered by way of Gov. Cuomo since New York was struck by the Coronavirus, was crucial. And by no doubt needed. By the effects it would play (Coronavirus) shortly after, what was also needed is for verification through our governing officials to put a stamp on things and keep schools closed - by given date- until further notice. And this new briefing became available by May 1.

On Friday, May 1, Gov. Cuomo ordered all schools in New York to be closed for the rest of the academic year. He even gave word that conventional classroom learning may not be back in time for the semester. Are we all ready for this? I'm sure students have no problem with it. Can you, as a parent, reason with this. To me it's times like this where family units are strengthened.

When you think about the amount of space a normal classroom takes up, doing feasible learning with social distancing while suited with a face mask is difficult. Even more, doing all this standing 6 feet apart. Guessing there was no way to reopen before the spring semester ends June 26.

The affect of this cancellation will play a toll on 4.2 million K-12, college, and university students. Maybe there's a good side to this. The combination of stay-at-home orders and the shutdown of school, I believe, will lunge in the minds of our young, forcing them to pry open a side to them they never saw. The negative side, now that they have this free time, how many will still be motivated to attend normal schooling knowing just how additional time can mold you.

A lot of these kids' parents who are subject to the real world are being trampled over morally. Millions of American workers terminated from work are now in the middle of dual fire. Either return to work and risk infection, losing unemployment benefits. As a whole, you could not be present at any age in America during these times without sacrificing something.

Where it lies very inconvenient is in states where governors have allowed businesses without social distancing restrictions to reopen. Waiters in businesses, for example, are very difficult to cater with social distancing guidelines.

A report came by the Labor Department as of April 30 stating that the businesses shutdowns and stay-at-home orders caused by the pandemic have led to 30 million Americans to file for unemployment insurance. Giving it more clarity 1 of every 6 workers. I didn't think or plan on being present in America during my lifetime with such stark statistics. One thing I have to credit Trump for in his background profile, he's the right man to turn this around. Given his prior career in analytically budgeting. Now that he's a president, who knows how urgent he is to fix things for the people.

Trump as a president, has his own way to address things. He went on by the last day of April, stating he believes the Coronavirus came from China's Wuhan Institution of Virology. When asked to give further cause, he shied away with no answer. To the date of this writing, I heard at least five different accusations to how the virus started. And I don't believe any.

The event of 9-11 had its share of speculation, which was very affirmative to who was truly responsible for the attacks. An event that causes more than quadruple more in fatalities, the cause may never subside, looking at things theoretically.

May, 3, 2020

New York City corona virus stats

Total cases: 166,883          Cases in last 24 hours: 2,378

Total deaths: 18,282          Deaths in last 24 hours: 51

Total hospitalized: 42,715

# Chapter 7

**Our experts silenced, experimental vaccine.**

Talk alone of reopening sounds good but is it promising. In times like this, I direct my trust to the experts. Especially with a disease that attacks with the speed of Coronavirus. It also should be noticed that at this given time, what lies deep within the mind frame of our governing body is now a relay of judgment by individual opinion. Scientists suggest one thing; politicians suggest something else.

This can be seen by how the Centers for Disease Control an Prevention graphed out an alternative for the nation to a safer reopening of businesses and institutions for the pandemic. Still, the white house blocked the expert's work to release them. America is about the value of the dollar. And it's sad people who were put in place for these purposes are being silenced.

Schumer said it himself that the nation deserves to have the advice of scientists, not politicians.

Yes, I favor Trump for tasks such as budgeting, but it's clear he's unfamiliar with medicine and science. At one given time during this outbreak, he advised the people to drink bleach as a remedy for the virus. Schumer gave another shot at Trump by saying this is the same man from his early claims that the Coronavirus would not be a problem, to also saying last month April that we have won the war against covid-19.

Times like this make me miss a more sound decision-maker like Obama. The question is, do we care more about lavish living or a safely governed environment for the people? By mid-March, America was documented as the only nation that began its reopening thru a rising death rate. Totally irresponsible judgment. If we don't make our people comfortable with judgment by our elected officials, we are weakening citizens' patriotic views and encouragement that they are in the hands of someone who cares for them.

Medical care surrounding the Coronavirus came in two forms treading down May. The good news is that a vaccine may possibly be on the way. The bad news Is a multisystem inflammatory syndrome in children that has been linked to Coronavirus has been discovered.

By this time frame, the bug had already killed 90,000 Americans. Health experts feared Without a vaccine, a second wave would almost be certain. Health arrived luckily through a biotech firm named Moderna based in Boston. What was proved in their behalf experimental vaccine had triggered immune responses in all healthy volunteers who were tested. A definitive experiment will later be tested in July, led by the U.S National Institutes of Health.

Due to the positive feedback, Wall Street soared, comprising there can be an early end to shutdowns and hysteria attributed to the bug. Moderna is just one of about a dozen companies in the race to engineer a vaccine.

When things couldn't get any worst, the city started investigating 145 possible cases of a potentially deadly syndrome linked to Cororavirus. The syndrome has only killed one five-year-old boy in the city and two more children statewide. Of 145 children in New York that were stricken by it, 67 tested positive for covid-19. I doubt that this will be a major concern being that the bug in its original state was here since February.

More and more signs that our elected officials favored reopening by means of certain metrics both excited me and scared me. Being a student of education I take the advice of our experts. America being under confinement without normal system of living is hard to bare. For now I hope those atop our government weigh every corner of a second wave occurring.

May, 18, 2020

New York City corona virus stats

Total cases: 190,408          Cases in last 24 hours :1,377

Total deaths: 20,720          Deaths in last 24 hours: 144

Total hospitalized: 50,120

# Chapter 8

## Minority communities, Why not reopen

On the other side of all the negative news on the Coronavirus, only 57 accounted deaths for the city of New York occurred as of Tuesday, May 19., Bringing the death toll to 20,934. That's great improvement Knowing where residents of the city evaded government collapse - with deaths ranging at 700 a day- all together with proper pursuit, the virus can be contained.

Before any hopes are raised low-income and minority communities need the utmost support as their neighborhoods are being be ravaged by the bug. By certain factors, their structure of residence provides low cover for a virus like Coronavirus. Public housing residences in more coherent terms. Just think about trying to social distance in an elevator or hallway.

Hearing the tribulations of how the virus targets certain levels of occupancy and shy away from others led me to believe this is better dealt with by military personnel. I say this mainly because of (1) the deaths fell stricken and (2) how strategically cunning you need to be to fight it. Our elected officials should be given credit for successfully containing this pandemic nationwide as a result of a reasonable portion of deaths occurring.

Studies administered still prove that about 27% of New York City's lower-income neighborhoods tested positive for covid-19 antibodies. While the general population is about 19%. The Bronx took on the highest percentage of positive tests at 34%.

A prior serviceman under Obama's cabinet spoke on this phase of the time we are entering as a binding of the peoples' phase. I agree the initial response to something like this event is more curiosity and shock. Those on the front line, as said by this serviceman, must summon the will to be diligent

The next list of advice I plan on documenting is revised but through mention of Shaun Donovan. Some are advocating for easing restrictions and reopening our economy now may, 22. To him, it was a mistake. To complete the job and struggle many on our front line encountered is to finish the job.

Progress bas been made in decreasing the amount of those infected and those that lost their lives. But here are three reasons we must still stand guard with proper restrictions surrounding Coronavirus.

(1)   Those that are undeserved have been hit the hardest. And were not yet suited for testing capacity as we enter a new low-level transmission. Still, the test and materials needed are minimum. You can't fight an enemy you cant see.

(2)   Tracing those infected is a must. So positive individuals, as well as their contacts who may have been infected, can take the steps they need to stay well.

(3)   We must remain [loose] for a second surge. Our hospitals are becoming less constrained, but we must have the capacity in place to respond effectively. Many New Yorkers cant quarantine at home. Hotel and wrap around services are becoming available, but we need to balance this before reopening.

Towards the end of May for inmates all throughout America I can assume that their main worry was for the wrong amount of people to be infected within their prison and be a sitting duck as the plague unfolded. My main fear was the spread of infection. Luckily in regards to my family back home there wasn't much mention of those more close them that were infected.

May, 24, 2020

New York City corona virus stats

Total cases: 194,667          Cases in last 24 hours: 716

Total deaths: 21,138          Deaths in last 24 hours: 52

Total hospitalized: 51,117

# CHAPTER 9

## George Floyd, Steps toward reopening,
## Summary of myself

While the plague that took the lives of already 400,000 worldwide and an event that puts shame to whoever yields a police badge and claims they are under police dignity to protect and serve took place. It was a foul, disgustful, and inhumane act that will, along with the Coronavirus, be a testimonial of torment

What occurred on Memorial Day was an incident through the hate of a black man in Minneapolis, in which an officer knelt on his neck for nearly eight minutes as he gasped for breath until he was pronounced dead. The man's name, George Floyd, left behind a loving family that was hurt by the killing of their gentle giant.

Police in Minneapolis, as of May 28 wished for everyone to remain calm while they built a criminal case. Two nights of dramatic protest following Floyd's death arose as Hennepin County Attorney Mike freeman who said they were following detailed planning to prosecute police officers for wrong use of deadly force.

The video was filmed by a bystander who watched hand-cuffed Floyd struggling while the white Minneapolis police officer Derek Chauvin, a 19-year veteran, used his knee to brutally press against Floyd's neck for eight minutes.

Uttering the same words, I can't breathe, which Eric Garner did before dying in Staten Island in 2014. The four officers at the scene of the incident were all fired. Rev. Al Sharpton and Gwen Carr, the mother of Eric Garner, got together and held a prayer in Minneapolis and requested the immediate arrest of all four officers.

Thankfully while America was under hypertension following the death of George Floyd, things were starting to sharpen up as a nation. Mayor DeBlasio estimated Thursday, May 28, that as much as 200,000 to 400,000 workers could come back to their jobs which was part of the first phase of the city's reopening.

He predicted by the first or second week of June, reopening could occur but has not announced a specific date. Reopening was said for my hometown to occur in three metrics on a downward trend formulized. At this given time, two of the three metrics were met. Businesses that were aimed to be the first phase of reopening are construction, manufacturing, wholesalers, and retailers. I stand by Mayor Oblasio's judgment. He has proven to be alert and a sound thinker. And I'm sure his board backing are fit and reliant for times like these. Politically speaking, me knowing the average American wouldn't defer opening and watch as the structure of our society is [still]. I'm thankful for all surviving Americans of these harsh times who made it this far. No matter what age, we all gave a contribution.

Speaking more on who put this writing together, my name is Raheem Cox. I'm a 32-year-old African-American man home in South Ozone Queens. As early as fifth grade is when I knew I had a skill for writing. Scoring the highest in the class on the reading city-wide test. Also throughout my years of schooling one of the prime areas I excelled in was writing reports. My father made sure from the age of 7 that me and my brother were the best of athletes.

In high school, I was the 2nd best sophomore in New York City on defense playing varsity football. From High school, between 18-21 I went on to college. I earned 32 credits but never finished completely. At the age of 22, I caught a reckless endangerment charge and was sentenced to 13-years.

Over my time in jail, I grew from a young adult to a full strong righteous man. I feel by all means that jail can make you or break you. And I feel that through all my time I spent before I had the strength to write this, I had no wonder I could turn my past faults into a credible work of literature. Stick by the moral I learned in prison, and you shall go far in life, "self-understanding defeats a perfect image."

At the end of May was just as much a strain for inmates especially black ones as it was for normal citizens who viewed the last minutes of George Floyd's life go to waste. I saw from in my cell on a news channel how some cops are still pent in days where blacks were treated less of a human being. And that racism discarded in this country after so many years of social and economic development is still a major issue in this country. Here at Elmira regarding corona is when the virus was introduced to these cell blocks and prison population full of prisoners that now had a new level of strain to endure. I can't determine why at Elmira it spread so quickly, but my correctional facility became the epicenter for infected cases months later. Frightening but true simultaneously to me writing this booklet the guy in the cell next to me had it.

May, 28, 2020

New York City corona virus stats

Total cases: 197,351                Cases in last 24 hours: 728

Total deaths: 21,362                Deaths in last 24 hours: 48

Total hospitalized: 51,380

# AFTERWORD

The big day was set for New York City, starting June 8. Defining the economic road to recovery. It will be a slight difference, though. Things won't be normal for the big apple but respect the progress. Mask and social distancing are still a must. The first phase will approve 400,000 people going back to work in the five boroughs.

Giving the order for five upstate regions to the second phase of reopening also. The final metrics include having enough hospital capacity, a backup supply of personal equipment, and strengthening the city's ability to test and trace cases of covid-19.

Thursday, May 30, 67 New Yorkers died, down from 700 deaths at the peak. I wrote this booklet in a tight corner, so give thanks for its completion. I hope it was informative through my minimum resources I had to put it together. We all shared a difficult moment in history. Feel free to recommend this to whoever wants it day by day. Week by weekly coverage of the first arrival of this virus to the reopening phase.

Recovery altogether months after the first reopening's unveiled a second wave for many states. As Joe Biden, our newly elected 46th president, was announced in December 2020. Americans saw the virus spread rapidly still. The good news is that a vaccine named Pfizer, which was said to be 95% effective, was on the market and being issued as the equalizer in the times facing this deadly disease. The first arrival of shipment was scheduled for December 12, 2020.

Experts say vaccine or no vaccine, the virus will be here for years to come. As of now any steps to shorten its effect is direly needed. I'm just thankful I had the motive to put this together. Make no mistake, jail is a very dangerous place. And know this for someone serving time; many find it impossible to bring forth such work."All confrontations with matter will be judged."

**VISIT**

<u>www.Rootforcepublications.com</u>

The # 1 author website in the U.S.

JOBS. BOOKS. PODCASTS.

**Root Force**
PUBLICATIONS

MENTAL HEALTH CONSULTATION.
COMMUNITY OUTREACH. LINKS.

BUY BOOKS WHOLESALE. CONSIGN.
CAREER COACHING.

OR

# BUY BOOKS VIA

## www.Rootforcepublications.com

**FIND YOUR NICHE**
Self-taught universal laws and
guidelines, by the remarkable author
Raheem Cox for finding one's niche

By: Raheem Cox

**The last question**
**?**

25 answers to your most
deeply thought questions

By: Raheem Cox

**25 OF THE GREATEST**
**NBA PLAYERS OF**
**ALL- TIME**

By: Raheem Cox

AMERICA POST
CORONA AND IN TO A
POSSIBLE TRUMP
RE-ELECTION

By: Raheem Cox

**TRIGGERED PERCEPTION**
HOW PERCEPTION IS USED TO
APPLY A FIXED AGENDA

HOW ARE AMERICANS HERDED ; FOOD
OUTLETS, POLICE DEPARTMENTS, THE
MILITARY

By: Raheem Cox

See the box

Countering the prison-style
assembly

By: Raheem Cox

**CRITICAL STANDPOINT**
Documentation On The Coronavirus
Coming From Two Epicenters

Classic edition
By:Raheem Cox

**WAR RECORD**
A comprehensive
visualization of America

By: Raheem Cox

FROM MENTALLY ILL

TO MENTALLY RICH

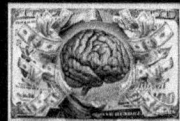

By: Raheem Cox

**THE FUDAMENTALS
OF MENTAL HEALTH
RECOVERY**

Raheem C

**CRITICAL STANDPOINT**
From nothing to something- A year
home from release

Classic edition
By:Raheem Cox

**THE BEGINNERS
GUIDE TO FILING
TAXES**

By: Raheem Cox

**NBA**

25 OF THE GREATEST NBA &
NFL PLAYERS OF ALL-TIME

**NFL**

By: Raheem Cox

**25 OF THE GREATEST
NFL PLAYERS OF
ALL-TIME**

By: Raheem Cox

**PURSUING MENTAL
DOMINANCE FOR THE
MENTALLY ILL**

By: Raheem Cox

www.ingramcontent.com/pod-product-compliance
Lightning Source LLC
Chambersburg PA
CBHW052106270326
41931CB00012B/2913